Original title:
Mad Love

Copyright © 2024 Swan Charm Publishing
All rights reserved.

Editor: Jessica Elisabeth Luik
Author: Linda Leevike
ISBN HARDBACK: 978-9916-86-068-7
ISBN PAPERBACK: 978-9916-86-069-4

Eclipsed by Passion

In twilight's embrace, desires ignite
Murmurs of longing, lost in the night
Lips converge under celestial beams
Whispers of love, woven in dreams

Hands intertwine, hearts synchronized
Burning emotions, no compromise
Stars bear witness to our fervent plight
As we become shadows in moonlight

Frenzied Hearts

Pulse of love, like wild rivers flow
Eyes that burn with an untamed glow
A dance of souls, in chaotic grace
Lost in the maze of each other's face

Embers flaring in passionate jest
Love unbounded, eternally blessed
Whirlwind emotions, we can't control
Two frenzied hearts, one fevered soul

Unhinged Affection

Love unrestrained, wild and mad
In each other's arms, we've always had
Moments of rapture, raw and surreal
Feelings too potent, we fiercely feel

Madness in love, no bounds we seek
Every touch sends a brilliant streak
In realms of passion, we dwell so deep
Unhinged affection, we vow to keep

Serenade of the Insane

A symphony played by lunatic hearts
Where sanity fades and true love starts
Notes of chaos, in tender refrain
A serenade sung by the insane

In madness we find our purest art
A song of love, tearing us apart
Dancing on the edge, we softly fall
United in madness, we conquer all

Untamed Hearts

In the wild where secrets start,
Whispers blend with nature's art.
Boundless skies, and silent cries,
We watch the dance of untamed hearts.

Freedom's call in twilight's hue,
Echoes deep, a love so true.
Beneath the stars, our spirits flare,
Where love unchains, beyond compare.

Rivers flow like passion's stream,
Dreams entwined in moonlit gleam.
Through forest deep and mountain high,
We chase where untamed hearts can fly.

Rapture's Frenzy

In the heat of fevered night,
Passion blazes, pure delight.
Bodies dance in rapture's fire,
Fusing flames of wild desire.

Eyes that pierce through veils of time,
Speak a language, pure, sublime.
Silent whispers, frantic tones,
Hearts beat like cascading stones.

Underneath the silver beams,
Love collides with fragile dreams.
In the chaos of our blend,
Find beginnings in each end.

Devoted Madness

Through the echoes of our years,
We've conquered pride, embraced our fears.
A love that twists through tangled maze,
In devotion's fervent, maddened blaze.

Eyes that see beyond the flaw,
Into depths where spirits draw.
Every scar becomes a mark,
Of our journey through the dark.

In the bedlam of our grace,
Find a world where we embrace.
No madness greater, no love as true,
Than the devotion shared by me and you.

Burning Vows

In the sacred vows we've spun,
Two hearts beat eternally as one.
Eyes that pledge, in fire and ice,
A covenant without a vice.

Through each trial and every storm,
In warmth of love, we keep so warm.
Promises like embers blaze,
Binding souls in endless daze.

Every moment, night and day,
Crafts our tale in shades of gray.
In the fervor of our vow,
We stand forever, here and now.

Inescapable Embrace

In twilight's soft and silent grace,
We find an inescapable embrace,
Where shadows dance and whispers play,
In the tender folds of a fading day.

The moonlight's kiss upon the sea,
Mirrors what our eyes can see,
Stars align in their secret chart,
Guiding the longing of the heart.

Moments slip through time's cold hands,
Leaving us in sunlit strands,
We grasp at dreams with fleeting might,
Hoping dawn will stretch the night.

In the hush of night's embrace,
We find our thoughts leave no trace,
Lost in a labyrinth of space,
Bound by time we cannot erase.

Yet in this dark, we find the light,
A spark that burns so pure, so bright,
In tenderness, we come to trace,
Our inescapable embrace.

Burning Whirlwind

Within the burning whirlwind's eye,
Flames lick the edges of the sky,
Fury swirls in a dance so wild,
In chaos, creation's undefeated child.

The wind sings songs of fierce delight,
Taming shadows with sheer might,
Whispering secrets in the blaze,
Tracing paths through fiery haze.

In this maelstrom, fierce and bold,
Stories of ancient times retold,
Ashes rise to kiss the stars,
Igniting dreams in broken jars.

Through the fire, our spirits fly,
On wings of strength, we touch the sky,
Burning souls, yet hearts set free,
In the whirlwind's fervent plea.

Embrace the storm, its vivid grace,
In its fury, find your place,
For in tempest, life's truths unspun,
In the burning whirlwind, we are one.

Forbidden Allure

In shadows where secrets lie,
Lustrous glance, a beckoning sigh,
Desire's whisper, hearts defy,
Silken threads where dreams untie.

Paths entwine where stars collide,
Hidden truths in eyes confide,
Yearning tides that can't abide,
In love's tempest, nowhere to hide.

Echoes dance through moonlit glades,
Passions pulsed in twilight shades,
Boundless nights and sweet cascades,
In forbidden allure, love invades.

Endless Craving

Hunger deep, a soul's unrest,
Thirsts unquenched by fate's bequest,
Restless heart in ceaseless quest,
Endless craving in love's jest.

Dreams that tease the weary mind,
Fragrant whispers left behind,
In your essence, peace I find,
Bound to you, my heart aligned.

Haunting melodies resound,
In your presence, all is found,
Love's sweet nectar so profound,
Captured by your soul unbound.

Raging Sentiments

Waves of fury, tempest born,
Crashing heart with vows sworn,
In the storm, love's bitter scorn,
Raging sentiments, hearts torn.

Eyes afire with endless blaze,
Passions trace through veils of haze,
In this ardor, lost in maze,
Burning bright, a fervent craze.

Ashes settle, embers gleam,
Silent whispers, love's quiet dream,
In the stillness, longing's theme,
Raging sentiments, hearts redeem.

Fevered Fancies

Visions weave through midnight's veil,
Phantom thoughts in moonlight's trail,
Love's sweet fever, hearts regale,
Fevered fancies never pale.

Eyes that sparkle, stars enshrined,
Dreams of you forever bind,
In this passion, solace find,
Hearts entwined, in love aligned.

Gossamer threads of tender grace,
In your love, a warm embrace,
Fevered fancies interlace,
In your presence, time's soft pace.

Carnal Whirlwind

Whispers in the night, bodies intertwine
Passion's fever hot, senses redefined
Lust's quicksilver dance, a wild design
In shadows deep and dark, desire's secrets shine

Hands tracing pathways, maps of flesh and sin
Heat between the lines, where lovers begin
A storm of touch and sighs, fire from within
Thrills of the unknown, unspoken akin

Breathless moments shared, where time distorts
In passion's grip we find our wild consorts
Whirlwind in our veins, electric retorts
Around and around, love's tempest transports

Tempestuous Affection

Your eyes, a storm in calm disguise
Thunder echoing in a lover's sigh
In the tempest's heart, where truths arise
Affection's lightning streaks across the sky

Waves of passion crash upon the shore
In our embrace, I crave nothing more
Shelter in your arms, where spirits soar
In tempest fierce, our hearts restore

Fire and rain in love's sweet serenade
A tumult wrapped in hues of soft cascade
In chaotic harmony, we have swayed
Tempestuous affection, never to fade

Manic Embrace

A whirlwind of thoughts, in love's boundless craze
Manic energy in your tender gaze
In the madness, we find our synaptic maze
Twirling in an uncharted, fevered daze

Hands grasp at hope, clinging to the night
Gravity defied in love's daring flight
Magnetic pulses draw our souls so tight
In the manic embrace, we find our light

In the chaos, hearts rapidly beat
Every touch ignites a burning heat
Through the frenzy, our spirits meet
In love's manic embrace, we are complete

Twisted Heartstrings

In the labyrinth of our souls, we twist
Heartstrings pulled by fate's unseen fist
Each tug a story in a lover's tryst
Bound together, in shadows kissed

Knots of memory, woven deep and tight
In love's fabric, complexities alight
Every glance a thread pulled into sight
In the twisted weave, we find our plight

With each pull, we draw closer or apart
A tapestry of love, sorrow and heart
In the tangled threads, we make our start
Twisted heartstrings, an intricate art

Wildly Entwined

In forests thick with ancient green,
We wove our dreams, unseen, serene,
Whispers danced on twilight's breath,
Binding close with fate's own weft.

Among the stars, our hearts took flight,
Caught in spirals, soft as night,
Twined with shadows, laced with light,
Melding warmth in darkest sight.

Paths that twined like rivers' flow,
Where vibrant pulses ebb and glow,
Silent echoes, soft and kind,
In nature's arms, so wildly entwined.

Rabid Yearnings

In the stillness of the night,
Burning with a fierce delight,
Echoes of a wild desire,
Set the shadows all afire.

Raging winds of worlds unseen,
Fan the flames of restless dreams,
Yearning's bite, both fierce and sweet,
Drives the pulse with frantic beat.

Unquenched thirst that gnaws within,
Spirit screams in wild din,
Boundless, raging, without end,
Till the dawn, our hearts defend.

Ecstatic Euphoria

Dancing 'neath the vivid skies,
Lost in laughter, bright as eyes,
Worlds collide in joyous glee,
Where the spirit's wild and free.

Mountains echo sounds of mirth,
Every breath a new rebirth,
Hearts that leap, surpass the bounds,
As the soul's delight resounds.

In the rhythm of the spheres,
We shed worries, doubts, and fears,
In ecstatic euphoria, fly,
To the apex of the sky.

Burning Illusions

In the flicker of the night,
Truths and dreams both take their flight,
Illusions dance in fire's glow,
Burning fierce, they come and go.

Reality, a distant shore,
Lost in dreams forevermore,
Shadows twist in fire's dance,
Calmly swaying in a trance.

Eyes that see the fire's light,
Gaze beyond the rim of night,
In the flames, our whispered confusions,
Fade away, as burning illusions.

Spirals of Lust

In shadowed nights and moonlit sheen,
Desires twirl in midnight's gleam.
Touch of fate in spirals thrust,
Hearts entwined in endless lust.

Whispers carried on the breeze,
To ignite forbidden pleas.
Breathless moments, time's unjust,
Lost together in this dust.

Fingers trace in fevered haste,
Chasing passion's fiery taste.
Echoed sighs, a lover's trust,
Craving more in spirals of lust.

Worlds collide, resistance fades,
Trust dissolves in love's cascades.
Flames that spark in moments' gust,
Forever bound in spirals of lust.

Batty Affection

In wooded glades where shadows rest,
A batty love begins its quest.
Wings of night in silent flight,
Seek the heart that beats with might.

Twilight whispers soft and low,
Chirps of affection softly flow.
In dusk's embrace where passion wakes,
A bond of love forever takes.

Guided by the moon's pale fire,
To realms where deep desires conspire.
Eyes that gleam in starlit dance,
Captured in romance's trance.

Across the night in fleeting gleam,
Together in a waking dream.
Bound by love in pure reflection,
Lost within this batty affection.

Wild Consummation

Through valleys green and mountains tall,
In passion's grip, we heed its call.
Wild hearts beat in untamed speech,
Desires soaring beyond reach.

In wilderness of night so vast,
Moments fleeting, holding fast.
Echoes whisper, soft elation,
In this wild consummation.

Embers burn in souls' bright flare,
A lover's touch beyond compare.
Nature's pulse in syncopation,
Dancing in this wild sensation.

Eyes that meet in morning's light,
Breathless joy in lovers' sight.
No restraint, just revelation,
Bound by wild consummation.

Haunted Seduction

Ghostly whispers fill the air,
In moonlit shadows, we beware.
A dance of souls in night's seduction,
Forever haunted by attraction.

Eyes that gleam with secrets deep,
In twilight's grasp, no longer sleep.
Touches that invoke induction,
Caught in haunted night's conduction.

Phantom hands in lover's plea,
Binding hearts in mystery.
Midnight's call in slow construction,
Lost in haunted seduction.

Invisible threads of fate entwine,
Souls that meet beyond design.
Eternal in their introduction,
Bound in haunted, sweet seduction.

Whirlwind of Hearts

In a dance of fate, we meet,
Twisting paths in chaotic beat.
Ancient whisper fills the air,
Love's tempestuous, without despair.

Embrace the storm and never flee,
Eyes locked, hearts wild and free.
In this whirlwind, we entwine,
Souls converging, time resigns.

Memories like leaves they'll blow,
Our whispered secrets, winds will know.
Each pulse a gust, each breath anew,
In love's storm, only truth will do.

Enraptured Fury

Firelights in starlit skies,
Passions burn through guarded lies.
Fleeting moments, heartbeats thrash,
Unseen marks, our spirits clash.

Vertigo from love's rampage,
Hearts untamed, refuse the cage.
In the storm, we find our peace,
Flames of fury never cease.

Ember eyes, a glance, they speak,
In shadows dark, our souls do peek.
Turbulence of fervor vast,
Together, we obliterate the past.

The Clamor of Eros

Amid the din of life we find,
An echo deep, a joyous bind.
Through tumult, chaos, there stands,
A love directed by unseen hands.

Silent whispers, roars within,
Through life's battle, love will win.
Tender glances, sparks ignite,
Met in noise, in hearts, light.

Laughter mingled, tears embrace,
In love's clamor, furrows erase.
Yearning shouts, its anthem clear,
Bound in passion, we persevere.

Untamed Romance

In fields of wild, untamed grace,
Two hearts find their dazzling place.
No restraints, just open skies,
Love's panorama, endless ties.

Breathless whispers on the wind,
Wild spirits, passions pinned.
Through the night, our paths align,
In wild love, pure and sublime.

Freed from chains, we boldly dare,
Soul to soul, stripped of care.
In this untamed, boundless land,
Together, wild loves we'll stand.

Wicked Affection

In shadowed corners, secrets lie,
A dance of whispers in the night.
The heart, entangled, beats so sly,
In wicked affection, lost in flight.

Eyes that glint with hidden fire,
Touch that warms a soul's deep core.
Every glance, a dark desire,
A love that always yearns for more.

Masks we wear, in moonlit glow,
Playing roles in twilight's play.
In wicked affection, tides do flow,
Binding hearts in a fervent sway.

Frenzied Hearts

Beneath the heavens' vast expanse,
Two frenzied hearts begin to dance.
Breathing in the cosmic chance,
Of love's wild and daring trance.

The pulse of life in hurried beat,
Their eyes connect in secret heat.
A world unknown beneath their feet,
In moments stolen, they discreet.

No cage can hold this fiery pair,
In the midst of chaos, unaware.
Frenzied hearts, beyond compare,
In their fervor, stripped to bare.

Whispers of Obsession

Hushed tones in the dead of night,
A whisper once, now strikes afright.
Obsession's call, its grip is tight,
Bound by thoughts that take to flight.

Eyes that follow every move,
In shadowed rooms, they slowly groove.
Echoes of a heart that prove,
Whispers linger, and they soothe.

A breeze that carries silent cries,
In hidden places, passion lies.
Obsession's whispers, truth denies,
In secret love where reason dies.

Chaotic Devotion

In realms where order bows to chaos,
Devotion blooms, entwined and lost.
A storm that rages, love embossed,
In fervent waves, its paths are crossed.

Eyes of fire, hearts ablaze,
In tumult's grip, they find their ways.
Chaotic dance in twilight's haze,
A fervor drawn from passion's gaze.

Each turn and twist, a tale of lore,
In chaos, finding love's sweet core.
Devotion strong, yet asking more,
Together, through the tempest's roar.

Kissed by Craziness

In shadows where the wild winds play,
We dance in dreams by night and day,
Touched by whispers, soft yet mad,
A kiss by chaos, fierce and glad.

Wild hearts in tempest, free to roam,
In every storm, we find a home,
Embraced by waves of sheer delight,
Craziness kissed under moonlight.

Eyes that glimmer with untamed fire,
Souls entwined in fierce desire,
Past the edge of sanity,
We find our sweetest clarity.

Laughter echoes in the dark,
We mark the night with every spark,
Lost in madness, but never lost,
Kissed by craziness, worth the cost.

The Heart's Frenzy

In the hush before the dawn,
The heart's frenzy lingers on,
Pounding rhythms, soft and wild,
In love's rapture, we are beguiled.

Under stars of silver flame,
Whispered words, electric claim,
Every beat a tender storm,
In this dance, the hearts are warm.

Caught between the night and light,
No shadows here, no sense of fright,
We chase the echoes of the heart,
Where frenzy ends, we cannot part.

Boundless skies and endless dreams,
Love's frenzy courses like swift streams,
Through valleys deep and mountains high,
Our hearts shall soar, and never die.

Uncharted Euphoria

Beyond the skies where hopes reside,
Uncharted euphoria, our guide,
We journey through the wild unknown,
With love as compass, hearts full-grown.

Stars like diamonds pave our way,
Dreams unfurl in the break of day,
In every touch, we find our call,
To realms where no shadows fall.

Boundless seas of light and grace,
In each other's arms, we trace,
Patterns of a world anew,
Where love's euphoria rings true.

Mountains tall and rivers wide,
Through joy and sorrow, side by side,
Uncharted paths we brave and own,
In euphoria, we find our home.

Love's Labyrinth

In the labyrinth of the heart,
Love's winding paths, a work of art,
Mystery in each twist and turn,
A flame that ever seems to burn.

Lost in corridors of delight,
Guided by the softest light,
We weave through shadows soft and fair,
Together, we are everywhere.

Walls of wonder, gates of dreams,
In every corner, passion streams,
We find each other, every time,
In word, in touch, in whispered rhyme.

Labyrinthine, yet crystal clear,
In love's embrace, we conquer fear,
Bound forever in this maze,
Love's labyrinth shall never glaze.

Devastating Allure

In whispers soft, you call my name
With every glance, ignites a flame
A siren's song, I can't ignore
The devastating allure I adore

Your eyes, two stars in endless night
A beacon's pull, a radiant light
Though storms may rage and oceans churn
For you, my soul will ever yearn

In shadows deep, your presence burns
A wild desire, the heart that learns
To dance upon this razor's edge
Where love and pain their vows have pledged

In moments fraught with tender fear
Your distant voice, I still can hear
A haunting echo, pure and true
The devastating allure of you

Fervent Turbulence

The winds of change, they howl and moan
A storm within, yet not alone
Through fervent turbulence we steer
Our hearts entwined, we conquer fear

In chaos found, a steady hand
Guides us through this shadowed land
With every trial, our spirits soar
Unbowed, unbroken evermore

A tempest fierce, our love sustains
In wild embrace, through joys and pains
A dance of flames, passion's might
Illuminates the darkest night

Together, we will face the storm
With fervent hearts, forever warm
Our love, a beacon bright and clear
In turbulence, we'll persevere

Unbound Hearts

In open fields where we run free
Unbound hearts, just you and me
No shackles hold, no ties that bind
Just endless skies and dreams we find

We chase the wind, embrace the now
Upon our brows, no heavy brow
With wings of hope, we soar above
Unbound hearts, in boundless love

Through valleys deep and mountains high
We journey on, no question why
For in our chest, a rhythm strong
The song of unbound hearts belongs

As rivers flow and seasons change
Our love remains, though lives estrange
Forever free, our spirits blend
Unbound hearts, a love that won't end

Electric Fever

In neon lights, we find our dance
An electric fever, by sheer chance
A touch ignites, a blinding flare
In pulses wild, we lay it bare

Your gaze, a spark in twilight's haze
A fevered dream in endless daze
Magnetic pull, no force denies
As we collide, electric skies

A current flows, in veins it runs
As bright as stars, as fierce as suns
In every kiss, a lightning's strike
Electric fever, love's delight

In nights alive with rhythmic beat
We lose ourselves in fevered heat
Entwined as one, no need for more
Electric fever evermore

Relentless Desire

Under twilight's gentle glow,
Yearning hearts begin to flow.
In the dark, we seek the light,
A fire burning through the night.

Whispers carried through the breeze,
Echoes from the rustling trees.
Passion's waves, they surge and crest,
In each heartbeat, we find rest.

Eyes that glimmer, touch that binds,
Relentless thoughts within our minds.
Dreams that form and take us higher,
Fueled by relentless desire.

Stars that twinkle overhead,
Guide us where our fates have led.
Unyielding flames in the soul inspire,
A never-ending, boundless fire.

Impetuous Love

Swift as winds that change the sky,
Impetuous love demands to fly.
Through moments brief, we find our wings,
In every touch, new promise springs.

Hearts collide like thunder's force,
Bonds unyielding, set their course.
Undeterred by time's decree,
In each other, we are free.

Spontaneous sparks ignite the dark,
Each heartbeat leaves an indelible mark.
Inside our souls, fires fiercely glow,
In impetuous love, we further grow.

Whirlwind passion, untamed and wild,
In each glance, a lover's smile.
Bound by the grace of skies above,
We revel in impetuous love.

Irresistible Obsession

In shadows cast by moonlit beams,
We chase the echoes of our dreams.
An irresistible pull we feel,
An obsession that seems so real.

Glimpses caught in fleeting light,
Draw us forth into the night.
Unseen forces, unseen hands,
Lead us through uncharted lands.

Eyes that pierce through veils of doubt,
In every whisper, every shout.
An endless search within the mind,
For something precious, hard to find.

Held captive by the unseen strings,
That guide our hearts to distant things.
Entrenched in endless fascination,
An irresistible sensation.

Berserk Tenderness

In the quiet of the dawn,
Love's sweet battle rages on.
With a fervor, pure and grand,
Hearts and souls in madness stand.

Tender touches, fierce embraces,
Hold us tight in boundless spaces.
Gentle whispers, shadows cast,
Tie us to the love that's vast.

Frenzy, passion intertwined,
Madly loving, undefined.
In the chaos, solace found,
Tenderness in madness bound.

Eyes that speak a thousand words,
Silent songs of hearts unheard.
Berserk tenderness reveals,
Love's wild truth, where nothing steals.

Passion's Labyrinth

In a maze of dreams we tread,
Where desires softly spread.
Whispers curl like vines around,
In this love, we are tightly bound.

Eyes speak what words can't say,
Hearts play in a tender fray.
Through twists of fate, we steer,
With every breath, you draw me near.

Stars align in secret code,
Guiding us on this hidden road.
Hand in hand, we explore,
This labyrinth offering more.

Each touch, a spark, ignites,
Turning shadows into lights.
Passion flows in every stream,
Bound forever in this dream.

Labyrinth of love profound,
In its depths, we are found.
Here we stay, lost in grace,
In passion's intricate embrace.

Unhinged Romance

Wild hearts in twilight's grip,
Yearning lips in shadows sip.
Midnight's whispers, secrets shared,
In this dance, we're unprepared.

Eyes meet in a fervent clash,
Unleashing love in a flash.
Bound by fate, yet defying,
In your arms, I'm flying.

Under moon's tender gaze,
Lost in this uncharted maze.
Embers stir with each caress,
In your touch, I find my breath.

Roaming through a stormy sea,
Unhinged love sets us free.
No rules, no chains, pure desire,
In your eyes, I see the fire.

Echoes of this wild romance,
In our souls, they eternally dance.
Unrestrained, forever known,
In your heart, my home is shown.

Inferno of Affection

Flames dance in the fervent night,
Hearts igniting, burning bright.
Eyes of tenderness catch fire,
In this blaze, our wild desire.

Heat that sears but doesn't harm,
Soundless cries, a soft alarm.
Bound in this intense embrace,
Lost in time, no need for grace.

From the ashes, love reborn,
Through the joy and silent mourn.
Every touch scorched with delight,
In this inferno of the night.

Breaths of warmth in coldest air,
Through this blaze, we boldly dare.
Inferno of emotions vast,
In your arms, my anchor's cast.

Hold me through this burning tide,
In your passion, I confide.
Inferno fierce, yet gentle too,
Wrapped in flames, yet warmed by you.

Wild Yearning

In the quiet of the night,
Wild yearning takes its flight.
Softest whispers fill the air,
Craving more than we dare.

Souls in harmony align,
Heartsbeat, echoing divine.
Through the echoes of desire,
Wild yearning sets us afire.

Eyes that gleam with hidden lust,
In your touch, a primal trust.
Lost in moments, time stands still,
Yearning wild, bending will.

Nature's call in every sigh,
Underneath the moonlit sky.
Raw and deep, a stirring quest,
In your closeness, I'm possessed.

Endless dreams we now pursue,
In this wild yearning true.
Bound by love's powerful force,
In your arms, my wild course.

Twisted Elegance

In shadows where the roses bloom,
Two hearts entwine beneath the moon.
A dance of dark, an elegant swoon,
Whispers echo in the silent room.

Fingers trace the lines of fate,
Silent vows in night's embrace.
A twisted path, yet hearts elate,
Love ignites in secret space.

Gilded masks of fervent dreams,
Glistening under twilight's gleam.
A phantom waltz, emotion streams,
Twisted elegance, a silent scream.

The night unfolds its darkened tale,
Elegance moves like wind-swept veil.
Underneath stars, vows prevail,
In shadows, love's secrets sail.

Pandemonium of Desire

A touch ignites the wildest fire,
In the pandemonium of desire.
Hearts entwine, sparks conspire,
Flames rise ever higher.

Eyes meet, electric gaze,
In passion's wild, unruly maze.
Yearning hands in fevered daze,
Moments blend in timeless haze.

Breaths collide in heated air,
Desire's chaos, stripped and bare.
Embers flicker, hearts ensnare,
In this pandemonium, pair by pair.

Waves of longing crash and break,
In love's storm, the earth does quake.
Desire's roar, each soul to shake,
Pandemonium in passion's wake.

Insatiable Quest

Across the lands and endless skies,
A heart embarks where dreams arise.
A journey bound by no compromise,
On an insatiable quest for the prize.

Through forests deep and mountains high,
Under the watchful, star-filled sky.
Seeks the soul without a sigh,
Ever onward, till hearts comply.

Faces met and paths unfold,
Stories shared, both young and old.
Every step, both sharp and bold,
On this quest, a love to hold.

A wanderer's heart, a seeker's soul,
Never resting, never whole.
In the quest, it finds its goal,
An insatiable journey to console.

Love's Anarchy

In the chaos of affection's reign,
Rules dissolve, like fleeting rain.
Love's anarchy, both loss and gain,
Hearts unbound, defy the chain.

Shattered norms like broken glass,
In love's rebellion, feelings amass.
Every moment, nothing's brass,
Time surrenders, free at last.

Passions flare in untamed flight,
Breaking barriers in the night.
Love's anarchy, the guiding light,
In its blaze, find pure delight.

Amidst the tumult, wild and free,
Hearts entwine in unity.
Love's anarchy, our decree,
Bound by chaos, eternally.

Torrid Whirlwinds

The desert sun ignites my soul,
A blaze that scorches, fierce and bright.
In torrid whirlwinds, we are whole,
Lost in the heat of day and night.

Beneath the sky, our shadows dance,
Mirages waltz across the sand.
In fervent gusts, we're in a trance,
Twined by a force we can't withstand.

The dunes arise like ocean waves,
In silent whispers, secrets told.
In torrid whirlwinds, we're both slaves,
To passion's fire, uncontrolled.

The storm may pass, the flames may die,
But embers in our hearts remain.
In torrid whirlwinds, we will fly,
Beyond the grasp of earthly plane.

Boundless Ardor

In endless skies, our spirits soar,
Across horizons wide and free.
Boundless ardor, forever more,
A love that's vast as open sea.

Our hearts, like stars, illuminate,
The darkest night with radiant glow.
In boundless ardor, we create,
A world where only we can go.

Through valleys deep and mountains high,
We journey onward, hand in hand.
In boundless ardor, we defy,
The limits time and space demand.

No chains to bind, no walls to climb,
Just endless fields where dreams are found.
In boundless ardor, lost in time,
Our love will evermore astound.

Chaotic Longing

A heart that beats in disarray,
Chaos reigns in every vein.
In fevered dreams where shadows play,
Chaotic longing, sweet and vain.

A symphony of shattered notes,
In dissonance, our souls collide.
Chaotic longing bravely floats,
On currents fast and wild, untried.

In stormy seas, our hopes align,
Though clashing winds may tear apart.
Chaotic longing, pure, divine,
A tempest bound within the heart.

The tethered strings of fate entwine,
With braids of yearning, fire-spun.
In chaotic longing, hearts combine,
Forever wild and never done.

Forbidden Rapture

In secret shadows, love concealed,
A rapture hidden from the light.
The whispers of our hearts revealed,
Only in the cloak of night.

A touch forbidden, sparks ignite,
In moments hushed, yet so intense.
Forbidden rapture takes its flight,
A love that's steeped in sweet suspense.

Through guarded doors and veiled dreams,
We steal a world that's echo-free.
In forbidden rapture's gleams,
We find the truth of what must be.

Though dawn arrives, the night may end,
Our secret stays, our hearts stay pure.
In forbidden rapture, we defend,
A love that's timeless, strong, and sure.

Devoted Delirium

In shadows deep where wonders sleep,
Whispers trace the moon's soft beam,
Hearts entwined in starlit night,
Drifting soft within a dream.

Echoes paint the twilight's hue,
In timeless dance of gleam and gloom,
Yearn and ache in silken thread,
Bound within love's tender loom.

Laughter lights the morning sun,
Casting off the night's embrace,
Souls aloft on wings of fire,
Lost within each other's grace.

Eyes alight with secret codes,
Silent truths that lovers speak,
Breaths entwined and hearts aligned,
Seeking where the shadows peak.

Dreams dissolve in waking dawn,
Yet leave a trace within the air,
Love's sweet scent, a lingering touch,
In devoted delirium, we dare.

Headlong Hearts

Cascade of stars in midnight's wake,
We plunge into the unknown deep,
Hearts that race and pulses quake,
Our very souls a sacred leap.

Eyes afire with untamed glee,
A journey where the wild things roam,
Hand in hand through restless seas,
Finding comfort in the storm.

Whispers in the gentle breeze,
Secrets shared in moonlit glow,
Headlong hearts without a pause,
In our embrace, the night does flow.

Daring winds weave dreams anew,
Wrapped in night's profound disguise,
We chase the dawn with whispered vows,
Clouds of fire in morning skies.

Timid sighs 'neath twilight's spell,
Songs of old in lover's lore,
Headlong hearts in fearless flight,
In each other, evermore.

Besieged by Passion

Thunder in the silent night,
Torches cast a fervent glow,
Passion's siege upon our hearts,
Flames of love begin to grow.

Eyes that spark with vibrant fire,
Lips that taste like aged wine,
Bound together in desire,
As day concedes to night's design.

Shadows dance in sultry air,
Breaths entwined as pulses race,
Besieged by passion's wild flare,
Each caress a fervent trace.

Torrid winds that fan the flame,
Waves of longing crash the shore,
In the throes of passion's game,
Hearts united, spirits soar.

Amid the storm, we claim the night,
Besieged by love's unyielding tide,
In fevered bliss, we find our light,
Within each other's gaze, we hide.

Infernal Tenderness

In the hearth of night's embrace,
Whispers warm the silent air,
Infernal in its tender trace,
Love's soft touch beyond compare.

Eyes that shine with embered light,
Hands that hold with gentle care,
In this glow, we find our flight,
Soaring high beyond despair.

Tender flames that lick the night,
Heat of hearts in whispered song,
Shadows cast in amber's sight,
In love's dance we do belong.

Holding tight as dawn draws near,
Infernal tenderness we share,
Gone the shadows, shed the fear,
In each moment, love lays bare.

Twining souls in sacred grace,
In fervent love we find our rest,
Infernal yet so soft the blaze,
Our hearts aloft, profoundly blessed.

Boundless Obsession

In shadows cast by moonlit gleam,
I wander through a ceaseless dream,
Endless thoughts, a boundless stream,
In search of what our hearts deem.

A whisper here, a touch so pure,
In every moment, love endures,
A captive of your sweet allure,
Through distant realms, my soul detours.

No cage can hold, no chain can bind,
An obsession knits us, heart and mind,
In hidden corners, love we find,
Our spirits twined, forever kind.

Boundless yearning, skies we chase,
In dreams we meet, and there embrace,
Together lost, in timeless space,
A fervent love, we can't erase.

Endless nights and days unfurled,
Through storms of life, our wings unfurled,
In boundless seas, our hearts are hurled,
Obsessed and free, within this world.

Unrestrained Passion

Fevered touches, burning bright,
In the darkness, pure delight,
A blazing fire, endless night,
Passion's glow, our guiding light.

Clandestine whispers in the wind,
Entwined spirits, hearts unpinned,
In fervent dance, we lose, we win,
In endless love, our lives begin.

Unbridled hearts, without a care,
Each breath, a tender, whispered prayer,
To realms unknown, we boldly dare,
Our passions fierce, beyond compare.

Eternal flames, we fan the spark,
In every kiss, ignite the dark,
Together soaring, leaving marks,
Our endless love, a radiant arc.

In wild embrace, our souls ignite,
A love unbound, a blazing sight,
In unrestrained, eternal flight,
We journey through the endless night.

Eccentric Affection

In curious ways, our love does grow,
Through twists and turns, to rivers flow,
A dance where only we can know,
Eccentric hearts, in softest glow.

Waltzing through the stars at night,
In laughter, tears, a boundless flight,
With colors bold, our love ignites,
A rainbow cast in love's own light.

Whimsical touches, tender sighs,
In every glance, a sweet surprise,
In eccentric love, we find the ties,
That bind us close, where true love lies.

Unorthodox, our tales unfurl,
In precious moments, pearls and swirls,
Together lost in love's wild whirl,
Embrace the storm, let winds unfurl.

With every beat, an endless stream,
Of love that weaves a vivid dream,
In eccentric ways, our spirits beam,
Affection found in love's grand scheme.

Rabid Revelry

In fevered nights, we wildly dance,
Our hearts engaged in fervent trance,
In rabid revelry, we glance,
At love that leaves us lost, entranced.

In chaotic rhythm, we explode,
Through wild embrace, our spirits flowed,
With reckless ardor, love bestowed,
In endless nights, our passion glowed.

No boundaries hold, no chains constrain,
In rabid fervor, joy and pain,
Through every storm, through sun and rain,
Together bound, in wild refrain.

Unchained hearts, in frenzied flight,
Through darkest hours, to dawn's first light,
In love's fierce grip, we find our right,
To revel through the boundless night.

In moments wild, in sweet delight,
Our love, a rabid, endless sight,
With passion fierce, our hearts ignite,
In revelry, through endless night.

Insane Cravings

In the still of the night, I dream,
Of flavors rich, a luscious scheme.
A passion deep, beyond mere taste,
An endless hunger through time and space.

Visions dance of sweet delight,
Every craving in my sight.
Insane desires I can't outpace,
Lost in indulgence, lost in grace.

Warm and tender, bold and sweet,
A craving never to retreat.
Frenzied heart, I can't deny,
These insane cravings will not die.

In chocolate rivers, I would swim,
In every bite, my senses brim.
Nights consumed by endless feast,
Insane cravings, never ceased.

An endless journey, wild and free,
A longing deep inside of me.
These insane cravings, fierce and true,
Capture my soul, through and through.

Ferocious Devotion

Through storm and fire, I persevere,
With ferocious devotion, sharp and clear.
No barriers can hold me back,
For love, relentless, nothing I lack.

In shadowed nights and brightest day,
A burning heart will find its way.
Ferocious love, it blazes strong,
In your arms is where I belong.

With every breath, with every beat,
My soul ignites, fierce and sweet.
Through turmoil, joy, and emotion,
I ride on waves of ferocious devotion.

Seas may rise, and mountains fall,
But love like this surpasses all.
A fire that roars, a passion bright,
Ferocious devotion through the night.

A journey endless, bound by fate,
A love that neither time nor hate,
Could ever dim, or scar, or break,
Ferocious devotion, for your sake.

Maddened Hearts

In tangled webs of fate, we meet,
Maddened hearts that fiercely beat.
A love so wild, it can't be tamed,
A passion roaring, both unashamed.

With eyes that burn like molten gold,
Our stories in each glance unfold.
Maddened hearts, no fear or doubt,
Together, we are fire drawn out.

In whispered dreams, we find our way,
Through shadowed night and dawning day.
Maddened hearts entwined as one,
A blazing star, a glowing sun.

We dance on edges, sharp and pure,
Where love's embrace is always sure.
Maddened hearts that never fade,
In each other's arms, we're unafraid.

A legacy carved in lovesick fire,
Our maddened hearts will never tire.
Bound in chaos, bound in flame,
Maddened hearts, forever claim.

Consumed by You

In every breath, your name I call,
In every whisper, I feel it all.
Consumed by you, in endless dream,
A passion strong, a living stream.

Your touch ignites a thousand fires,
Fueling all my deep desires.
Consumed by love, I drown in bliss,
Lost in the warmth of your sweet kiss.

In every glint, your eyes bestow,
A universe I long to know.
Consumed by you, I cease to be,
I'm only us, eternally.

Your voice, a melody, divine,
In every note, your heart in mine.
Consumed by moments, precious few,
Lost and found, consumed by you.

In timeless dance, our souls confide,
With every heartbeat, side by side.
Consumed by love, by hope, by grace,
Forever locked in your embrace.

Riotous Passion

In hearts alight with fervent fire,
Midnight whispers coltish ire.
In a dance of souls entwined,
Unseen boundaries we unwind.

Rushing waves of wild delight,
Love's tempest, fierce and bright.
Bound by flame, our spirits soar,
Beyond tomorrow, evermore.

Storms in silence oft conceal,
Truths that burning hands reveal.
In the dark, we find our ceaseless blaze,
Echoes of our riotous days.

Fierce and fervent, raw desire,
Veins imbued with wild pyre.
Passion's tempest we uphold,
Riotous beauty unrolled.

Emerald eyes and raven hair,
Whispered secrets, hearts laid bare.
Through the tempest, through the roar,
Riotous passion, evermore.

Inescapable Infatuation

In shadows deep, where dreams take flight,
A whisper calls from endless night.
Inescapable, the siren's song,
In hearts where fiery passions throng.

Gaze upon a moonlit hue,
Eyes that pierce the soul anew.
Bound by chains of sweet elation,
Sworn to this infatuation.

Silken words in midnight's veil,
Echoes of an olden tale.
Through the storm, against the tide,
Inescapable, love's relentless stride.

Caught within this tender snare,
Breathless moments we declare.
Martyrs of our own creation,
To inescapable infatuation.

Endless nights and crimson dawn,
Each new day, a passion drawn.
In a realm of dream's sensation,
Lives our inescapable infatuation.

Blazing Fascination

Stars above and fires below,
In your eyes, desires grow.
In a dance where sparks ignite,
Blazing through the endless night.

Fingers trace the heart's design,
In your touch, a mystic sign.
Whispers soft in fascination,
Love's profound and fierce creation.

Eyes that shine with secret light,
Flame and shadow in the night.
In a gaze so captivating,
Blazing hearts, forever mating.

Boundless skies and endless seas,
In your soul, the world I seize.
Fascination bold and bright,
Guides us through this ardent flight.

From the ashes, soaring high,
Wings of flame towards the sky.
Blazing hearts with no cessation,
Lost in endless fascination.

Wicked Devotion

In your eyes, a wicked gleam,
Tales of love and darkened dream.
Bound by chains of raw emotion,
Lost in endless, wild devotion.

Whispers low in haunted night,
Touch of flame and fierce delight.
Darkness holds our secret, dear,
Devotion wicked, without fear.

In the shadows, passions burn,
Souls entwined and hearts that yearn.
Through the tempest, wicked fashion,
Our devotion, fierce compassion.

Bound by fate, our souls adhere,
In the dark, our truth sincere.
Tales of wild and haunted potion,
Wicked, endless, fierce devotion.

In the dawn's soft, tender light,
Break the chains that bind us tight.
Wicked love in full emotion,
Lost in endless, deep devotion.

Boundless Desire

In the vast expanse of the starry sky,
Dreams take flight on wings of fire,
Heartbeats align, breaths synchronize,
Endless echoes of boundless desire.

Whispers ride the night's cool breeze,
Melding spirits, unseen but near,
Eyes locked under cryptic keys,
In this chase, there's nothing to fear.

Moonlit paths weave tales untold,
Stardust cloaks our every sigh,
In this boundless grip, we fold,
Hearts coalesce, we fly so high.

Desires churn like ocean tides,
Unseen currents, pulling strong,
In their swell, the soul confides,
A boundless rhythm, an endless song.

Embraced by dreams that never tire,
In twilight's arms, we find our place,
Touched by endless, boundless desire,
We merge as one in timeless space.

Turbulent Affection

Through storms of love, we navigate,
Hearts adrift on waves so high,
Affection's pull we can't negate,
In turbulent seas, together we fly.

Raging winds, they bend and break,
Still, we tether, holding tight,
In every tempest, love we stake,
Guiding stars in the darkest night.

Emotions crash like thunder's roar,
Yet in chaos, we find peace,
Drawn together even more,
Bound by love that shall not cease.

Through tempest's rage and blinding rain,
Navigating with hearts so true,
Every touch, a kindred gain,
Turbulent affection, tried and new.

United in tumultuous skies,
Love's fierce wind, our guiding light,
Affection forged where turmoil lies,
In every storm, love's pure delight.

Lunatic Embrace

Under the mad, capricious moon,
We dance in shadows, bathed in light,
Lunatic embrace, our hearts attune,
To rhythms wild, beyond the night.

Echoes of laughter, whispers soft,
In midnight's hold, our souls we find,
Crazy love, our hearts aloft,
In lunatic whims, our lives enshrined.

Stars may fade, and moons may wane,
But our embrace defies the time,
Bound by madness, freed from pain,
In every pulse, a love sublime.

Chasing dreams through endless skies,
Hand in hand, a wild ballet,
Through the night, our spirits rise,
In lunatic embrace, we'll stay.

With each turn, we twist and fall,
Ecstasy in every trace,
Madly bound, through it all,
In this lunatic, endless embrace.

Savage Longing

In the depth of night's dark hold,
Savage longing burns so bright,
Passions raw, untamed, uncontrolled,
In fierce embrace, we find our light.

Echoing cries reach through the void,
Primal hearts, a fire ignites,
Beyond the world's facade, we're toyed,
In savage throes, our soul delights.

Wilderness within our gaze,
Eyes that pierce the silent dark,
Every touch, a tender blaze,
In longing's wild, we leave a mark.

Feral whispers fill the air,
Nature's call, a siren's song,
Through the savage night, we dare,
To find a place where we belong.

Untamed spirits, fierce and strong,
Bound by something wild and free,
In savage longing, hearts prolong,
An endless search through destiny.

Immortal Yearning

In shadows deep, where whispers play,
Immortal dreams begin to sway,
A heart that beats beyond the night,
Holds secrets of an endless light.

Ancestral echoes gently call,
Through ancient woods and whispers small,
A spirit seeks what cannot die,
In realms where stars forever lie.

Time bends and twists, its endless flow,
In labyrinths where silence grows,
Yet yearning lives, a fervent flame,
For love immortal, whispers name.

Beneath the moon's eternal gaze,
Across the nights and countless days,
A path unwinds in silver threads,
Where longing walks and softly treads.

In quiet dreams, the soul takes flight,
To dance with phantoms in the light,
For immortality's gentle kiss,
Awaits in realms of endless bliss.

Martian Romance

Under the red and mottled sky,
Two hearts on Mars dare to defy,
Space and time, they intertwine,
In whispers of a love divine.

Amidst the dust and endless plains,
Where ancient rivers left their stains,
A blush of love's first coy embrace,
A tale unfolds in alien space.

The stars above, a silent choir,
Ignites their hearts with cosmic fire,
For even here, where planets drift,
Love's tender touch becomes their gift.

Through glassy domes, they gaze in awe,
At desolation's grand tableau,
A newfound world, both strange and wild,
Yet love persists, untamed, beguiled.

Beyond the cratered, arid lands,
They walk together, hand in hand,
For Martian nights, beneath the stars,
Hold secrets of their love afar.

Purgatory's Kiss

In twilight hues, where shadows cling,
Purgatory's whispers bring,
A kiss that lingers, soft and brief,
Amidst the dance of silent grief.

Between the worlds, a place of woe,
Where spirits wander to and fro,
In search of peace, redemption's grace,
In haunting, spectral interlace.

A fleeting touch, both chill and warm,
Through limbo's haze and shifting form,
Promises of what could be,
In realms beyond our sight to see.

Yet here they stay, in endless dream,
Caught between the realms, unseen,
For purgatory holds them tight,
In shadows of eternal night.

With every sigh, a hope released,
Of finding solace, final peace,
In purgatory's soft caress,
Awaits the kiss of sweet excess.

Frenzied Courtship

In candlelight's soft, flick'ring glow,
Two hearts entwine, a fiery show,
Frenzied whispers, breaths collide,
In a dance where passions glide.

Eyes locked in a tempest's swirl,
A storm of love begins to whirl,
Where every touch, electric, keen,
Embodies all the in-between.

In midnight's hush, they find their way,
In frenzied courtship's wild ballet,
Entwined in throes of pure delight,
They dance amidst the velvet night.

Recognition in a glance,
Their souls entwine in mystic dance,
Unspoken words, a binding vow,
To love's allure, they both avow.

Endless rapture, lover's flight,
They soar within the shadowed night,
For frenzied hearts will never tire,
In passion's grasp, they'll blaze in fire.

The Blaze Within

Within the heart, a fire roars
Through endless nights and sunlit shores
A spark that grows, ignites the soul
To reach beyond, to grasp the goal

Embers dance in gilded light
A beacon through the darkest night
Desires fierce, we chase, we yearn
In passion's flame, we twist and turn

The blaze within, an ardent call
That fuels our rise, prevents our fall
A pyre of dreams, it lights our way
Guides us through both night and day

Tempestuous Harmony

In stormy skies the thunder roars
Waves crash upon the distant shores
A symphony of nature's might
Where chaos reigns, yet brings delight

Winds that howl and clouds that weep
Create a melody so deep
Within the tempest, notes align
In disarray, a rhythm fine

Tempestuous harmony unfolds
A wild heart it gently holds
In every storm, a song is found
In nature's fury, love is bound

Infernal Affection

In flames of love we find our fight
Where shadows dance in fervent light
An ardor burning deep within
Where every touch is born of sin

Infernal whispers, fiery gaze
A passion set in ardent blaze
Hearts consumed in molten fire
A dance upon a pyre of desire

In embers' glow, we fuse as one
A love that cannot be undone
Infernal affection, wild and free
A bond that scorches, endlessly

Heat of the Moment

In fleeting seconds, worlds ignite
A flash of passion, pure delight
Eternal moments in a glance
A timeless waltz, a daring dance

Heat of the moment, hearts afire
In waves of fervor, we aspire
To seize the day, to own the night
In blazing love, we take our flight

Flames that flicker, never fade
Our love eternal, unafraid
In every heartbeat, moments keep
A timeless bond, forever deep

Enchantment's Grip

In twilight's hush, the magic weaves,
Through silent woods, past ancient leaves,
A whispered spell, the heart receives,
In shadows deep, the soul believes.

Moonlight dances on cobbled lanes,
Mystic call in silver chains,
Whispers call from distant plains,
Enchantment's grip, the spirit claims.

Stars align, their secrets shared,
In night's embrace, all dreams are bared,
Through time's veil, the heart prepared,
Enchantment's grip, forever dared.

In twilight's weave, the tale unfolds,
Through twilight's art, the heart remolds,
Mystic lands, where time withholds,
In shadows deep, the soul beholds.

Ancient echoes, softly speak,
Through silent woods, secrets seek,
In twilight's hush, no longer meek,
In shadows deep, enchantment's peak.

Delirious Desire

Flames ignite in secret glance,
Passion stirs in mystic trance,
A touch, a spark, a wild dance,
Delirious desire's vast expanse.

Eyes meet, a fire untamed,
In heat of night, the souls proclaimed,
Boundless paths, no need for names,
Delirious desire, burning flames.

A whisper soft, a breath so near,
In shadows close, no place for fear,
Bound by longing, hearts adhere,
Delirious desire, crystal clear.

Through endless dreams, the moments blend,
In ardent plea, the bodies tend,
Together bound, no need to mend,
Delirious desire, no end.

In fevered night, the world aside,
By passion's tide, in stealth we ride,
Through whispers bold, a love implied,
Delirious desire, hearts collide.

Forbidden Fever

In moonlit shade, where shadows meet,
A fervent pulse, a heartbeat's beat,
A secret path, where silence speaks,
Forbidden fever's hidden peaks.

Eyes that hide beneath the veil,
Soft whispers trace a lover's tale,
In hush of night, emotions sail,
Forbidden fever, hearts prevail.

Touch of silk in phantom light,
In clandestine, seductive flight,
A rush of blood, a burning sight,
Forbidden fever, pure delight.

Through veiled routes, our spirits bind,
In passion's quest, no trail behind,
A daring dance, the stars aligned,
Forbidden fever, undefined.

In breathless grace, we intertwine,
A hidden pledge, a secret sign,
Bound by fate, our souls enshrined,
Forbidden fever, love divined.

Tempestuous Yearning

In storm's embrace, where wild winds howl,
A longing deep, within hearts prowl,
Through thunder's roar and nature's growl,
Tempestuous yearning, a fervent vow.

In lightning's flash, the eyes collide,
Through rain's caress, the secrets hide,
A longing fierce, no storm can bide,
Tempestuous yearning, side by side.

In swirling mists, our essence flies,
A storm of passion, where truth lies,
Through tempest's eye, beneath the skies,
Tempestuous yearning, never dies.

The ocean's rage, the tides of fate,
In nature's arms, we navigate,
A journey wild, where hearts elate,
Tempestuous yearning, contemplate.

In tempest's wrath, a love reborn,
Through chaos fierce, the bond is sworn,
In nature's wild, our souls adorn,
Tempestuous yearning, evermore.

Raging Desires

In the shadows, flames ignite,
Passion's storm, a restless night,
Eyes that burn with wild fire,
Hearts entwined in deep desire.

Whispers fill the starlit air,
Promises, a lover's dare,
Heat that sears the very soul,
Two halves striving to be whole.

Tangled paths where dreams collide,
Waves of longing, vast and wide,
Breathless moments, stolen sighs,
Future written in our eyes.

Fiery pulses, keen and bright,
Craving touch beneath the light,
Endless dawns and dusky eves,
In love's arms, the soul believes.

Raging desires, burning deep,
Memories that we will keep,
Torrid dance of heart and mind,
In this blaze, our souls entwined.

Fiery Obsession

Flames of lust, they scorch the night,
Illumined shadows trembling bright,
Eyes that pierce through darkened veils,
Endless whispers, endless tales.

Torn between what's wrong and right,
Yearning fuels the fiercest fight,
Hands that grip with fevered might,
Bodies locked in love's own rite.

Eyes aflame with hidden fire,
Silent screams of deep desire,
Unseen bonds that hold us tight,
Lost in passion's harrowing height.

Echoes of a lover's cry,
Touch that leaves the soul awry,
In the smolder of the past,
Burning love, forever cast.

Fiery obsession, fierce and wild,
Two souls, turbulent and riled,
In the embers of the night,
We are scorched by love's delight.

The Siren's Embrace

Across the boundless, churning seas,
Her calls drift on the midnight breeze,
Eyes like stars in ocean's night,
Luring souls to hidden light.

In her song, sweet dreams resound,
Soft whispers in the deep profound,
Hearts entranced by lilting grace,
Drawn into the siren's embrace.

Ghostly waves and mirrored skies,
Underneath her haunted eyes,
Distant shores are lost from sight,
To her spell, all hearts take flight.

Yearning pulls beneath the foam,
Lost in dreams far from home,
In her arms, we find our place,
Cloaked within the siren's embrace.

Through the years and endless tides,
Love's sweet ache, it never hides,
Waves of longing, swift apace,
Eternal in the siren's embrace.

Lunatic Yearnings

Underneath the moon's pale glow,
Whispers drift where shadows go,
Haunted eyes and restless hearts,
Broken dreams, where madness starts.

Star-crossed souls, they chase the night,
In their search for lost delight,
Lunatic yearnings, fierce and wild,
Haunt the lovelorn, like a child.

Secrets held beneath the stars,
Echoed cries from distant scars,
Phantom hopes that weave and twine,
In the dark where hearts align.

Moonlight guides us, lost and frail,
Through the night's deceptive veil,
Bound by chains of shadows vast,
Yearning for a peace at last.

Lunatic dreams, forever yearn,
In the night, their embers burn,
Heartfelt cries, devoid of light,
Shining bright in endless night.

Fierce Enchantment

In the mystic twilight's breath,
Stars rise in fierce motion,
Whispers of a spellbound depth,
Bind the heart's devotion.

Embers dance in dusky skies,
Flames of ancient dreams,
Silent echoes where truth lies,
In the moonlit streams.

Veils of night, secrets spin,
Enigmas softly spoken,
Waves of fate, the soul within,
Wholly unbroken.

The tempest roars, wild and free,
A symphony so grand,
In this fervent, deep decree,
Fates conspiracies planned.

Winds of change through time they sweep,
Magic's deep caress,
By the storm we dare to keep,
Lost in fierce enchantress.

Obsessive Delight

In the heart where shadows play,
Lies an endless yearning,
Passions rise with break of day,
Set the world a-burning.

Eyes that haunt, a glance divine,
See me in the night,
Sacred secrets fall in line,
Obsessive pure delight.

Echoes call from silent halls,
Desires never rest,
Through the veil, as darkness falls,
Acerbic in our quest.

Crimson skies in morning's light,
Bound by what is right,
Still we chase the endless sight,
Of pleasure, fierce and bright.

In the silence, voices loud,
Dreams are held so tight,
Hidden in the darkest shroud,
Obsessive, true delight.

Frenetic Adoration

In the chaos of the soul,
Rising tides of passion,
Seeking truth within the whole,
In scattered, wild fashion.

Heartbeat racing, lost in time,
Moments of elation,
Chasing love, a steep incline,
Frenetic adoration.

Whispers loud in crowded room,
Secrets left unspoken,
Every touch dispel the gloom,
Binding hearts unbroken.

Skies alight with fervent flame,
Shadows dance in light,
Lost within this wicked game,
Love's chaotic fight.

Endless nights in fervor's grip,
Star-crossed consternation,
On the edge we always slip,
Frenetic adoration.

Ceaseless Yearning

In the still of twilight's hold,
Dreams of you remain,
Wandering through paths untold,
Through love's sweet refrain.

Longing whispers in the night,
Endless, soft and deep,
Chasing shadows in the light,
Where our secrets sleep.

Stars align to guide the way,
Hearts beat in the dark,
Lost within the wordless sway,
Soul's eternal spark.

Waves of time that crash and roar,
Destiny unfolds,
Yet through every distant shore,
Ceaseless love beholds.

In this journey, no return,
Paths that never end,
Through the fire, we still yearn,
For love's true transcend.

The Ties That Blaze

In the hearth of hearts, a fire grows,
A flame that neither wanes nor slows.
Through trials and time, it fiercely glows,
A beacon where our every passion flows.

Bound by sparks, we dance in light,
Two entities enshrined in sight.
With every ember, love ignites,
Turning darkness into bright.

In shadows long, the fire remains,
Unyielding through the storms and pains.
Its warmth, in marrow, it sustains,
A tether strong in ardent veins.

Thus, through the years, the blaze endures,
A timeless bond that fate assures.
No force on earth this love immures,
Eternal as the stars and moors.

Inferno of Souls

In realms where spirits freely lose,
A conflagration born of muse.
Bodies melt in molten hues,
An inferno none refuse.

In fevered pitch, our echoes meld,
Where haunting flames are softly held.
Through pyres of thoughts profoundly swelled,
Our every fear and joy are quelled.

In brazen heat, we form our creed,
An oath to scars and hearts that bleed.
With every spark, we feed the need,
To rise as one, forever freed.

From embers rise, renewed, confined,
In raging bonds that fiercely bind.
Transcending time, and space, and mind,
Inferno of souls, deeply entwined.

Ecstatic Madness

In realms where sanity unravels,
Through twisted paths our spirit travels.
In shadows deep, where reason marvels,
Madness sings, and sense it baffles.

The siren song of lunacy calls,
In vibrant halls, where silence falls.
Dancing through time in echoing walls,
Lost in thrill, as sanity stalls.

Ecstatic tremors seize the mind,
Waves of euphoria, souls will find.
Where chaos and calm are intertwined,
In madness, every truth's defined.

With every pulse, the heart inflates,
Through madness, joy illuminates.
In spirals wild, our fate awaits,
Ecstatic madness—heaven's gates.

Storm-touched Lovers

Beneath a sky where thunder tears,
Two souls unite in whispered prayers.
In tempest fierce, their passion flares,
Bound by storm, their burden bares.

Their hearts, electrified and bold,
Find refuge from the biting cold.
Through rain and wind, their truths unfold,
In love profound, their fears consoled.

The lightning marks their fervent kiss,
A union forged in tempest's bliss.
No force of nature could dismiss,
The storm-touched bond that persists.

As heavens roar and skies reclaim,
Their love remains, an endless flame.
In every storm, they stake their claim,
Two lovers' hearts, one surname.

Pulsing Chaos

In the heart of night's deep thrall,
Moonlight fades and shadows sprawl,
Winds of fate in silence call,
Whispers fierce but soft withal.

Mid the storm, our spirits play,
Lost along some shrouded way,
Guided by the dawning ray,
Light amidst the wild Friday.

Every breath a fleeting chance,
In the whirl of fate's wild dance,
Unseen forces from the glance,
Shape our lives, devoid of stance.

Chaos pulses, heartbeat's tread,
In the dreams where hopes are fed,
Paths we walk are loosely fed,
By the choices overhead.

Here within the starlit night,
Amidst the dark, amidst the light,
We find purpose, burning bright,
Navigating chaos's flight.

Abyss of Devotion

Eyes that meet on tender ground,
Silent whispers, hearts unbound,
Love that's lost and yet profound,
In the void where souls are found.

Depths of longing, endless sea,
Where devotion yearns to be,
Unseen ties in mystery,
Binding you and binding me.

Every kiss a stolen time,
Echoes through a realm divine,
In our hearts, the night chimes,
Love's devotion, crystal shine.

Years may fade and moments pass,
Glass of time both slow and fast,
In the abyss, shadows cast,
Love remains, an endless vast.

Hold me close as stars align,
Hearts entwined, a sacred sign,
In the dark our souls refine,
Abyss of devotion, ever mine.

Tangled Tempests

Torn by winds of restless might,
Skies are dark, devoid of light,
In the storm's fierce, wild flight,
Hope still whispers, faint and bright.

Through the tempest's tangled veil,
Ships of dreams sail strong and frail,
Guided by a fervent tale,
Braving winds and moments pale.

Thunder roars, the heavens break,
Earth and sky begin to shake,
In our hearts, the storms awake,
Strength we find, no fear to quake.

Paths entwined in life's vast maze,
In the chaos, moments blaze,
Through the tempests, endless days,
Love shall find its steadfast gaze.

As the storm begins to die,
Clearer hopes on brightened sky,
In the calm where dreams can fly,
We find peace, and questions, why.

Dizzying Emotions

In a swirl of fleeting dreams,
Life flows onward, like the streams,
Caught in dizzying extremes,
Silent truths and hidden schemes.

Hearts that flutter, unsure beats,
Moments sweet, yet incomplete,
Love's a dance on restless feet,
In the swirl where shadows meet.

Emotions strong, complexities,
In your eyes, the galaxies,
Held in time's uncertainties,
Yet embraced in fantasies.

Joy and sorrow, intertwined,
In the present, future's mind,
Keep us steady, moments find,
Through the chaos, love is blind.

Dizzying rush, hearts break free,
In your arms, eternities,
Whispered hopes and reveries,
Dizzying emotions, me and thee.

Milton Keynes UK
Ingram Content Group UK Ltd.
UKHW050131270624
444593UK00005BA/62